# TRUCK AND TRACTOR PULLS

BY KATE MIKOLEY

Gareth Stevens
PUBLISHING

Please visit our website, www.garethstevens.com. For a free color catalog of all our high-quality books, call toll free 1-800-542-2595 or fax 1-877-542-2596.

**Cataloging-in-Publication Data**

Names: Mikoley, Kate.
Title: Truck and tractor pulls / Kate Mikoley.
Description: New York : Gareth Stevens Publishing, 2020. | Series: Motorsports maniacs | Includes glossary and index.
Identifiers: ISBN 9781538240984 (pbk.) | ISBN 9781538241004 (library bound) | ISBN 9781538240991 (6 pack)
Subjects: LCSH: Tractor pulling (Motorsports)--Juvenile literature. | Truck driving--Competitions--Juvenile literature.
Classification: LCC TL233.3 M63 2020 | DDC 796.7--dc23

First Edition

Published in 2020 by
**Gareth Stevens Publishing**
111 East 14th Street, Suite 349
New York, NY 10003

Copyright © 2020 Gareth Stevens Publishing

Designer: Sarah Liddell
Editor: Kate Mikoley

Photo credits: Cover, p. 1 angel217/Shutterstock.com; dirt background used throughout Yibo Wang/Shutterstock.com; tire mark texture used throughout Slay/Shutterstock.com; pp. 5, 11 Keith Bell/Shutterstock.com; p. 7 Royalbroil/Wikimedia Commons; p. 9 Delmas Lehman/Shutterstock.com; p. 13 JimboMcKimbo/Shutterstock.com; p. 15 Gestur Gislason/Shutterstock.com; p. 17 Belish/Shutterstock.com; pp. 19, 21, 27 Peter Braakmann/Shutterstock.com; pp. 23, 29 MediaNews Group/Boulder Daily Camera via Getty Images/Contributor/MediaNewsGroup/Getty Images; p. 25 Gbcue/Wikimedia Commons.

Printed in the United States of America

CPSIA compliance information: Batch #CS19GS: For further information contact Gareth Stevens, New York, New York at 1-800-542-2595.

# CONTENTS

# SUPER STRENGTH

Trucks and tractors are strong. Tractors are often used on farms to pull other farm tools. Some trucks pull cars behind them! Truck and tractor pulls are **competitions** in which these **vehicles** pull heavy loads to see which is the strongest.

# TEST DRIVE

TRUCK AND TRACTOR PULLS ARE
OFTEN HELD AT COMMUNITY FAIRS.

# HOW IT WORKS

In truck and tractor pulls, each vehicle is fixed to another machine called the sled. On the sled is a weighted box. As the sled is pulled, the box moves closer to the truck or tractor. This makes it harder to pull as time goes on.

SLED

# TEST DRIVE

## THE TRUCK OR TRACTOR THAT PULLS THE SLED THE FARTHEST WINS!

As the vehicle starts to pull the sled, the front wheels often come off the ground. Once this happens, the **steering wheel** isn't much help. Instead, drivers commonly direct the vehicle using two brake pedals, or levers pressed by the feet.

# TEST DRIVE

ONE OF THE BRAKE PEDALS CONTROLS THE
LEFT BACK WHEEL AND THE OTHER CONTROLS THE
RIGHT BACK WHEEL. THE DRIVER CAN STEER BY USING
THE BRAKES ON ONE WHEEL OR THE OTHER.

# IN CONTROL

The person driving the truck or tractor is not the only driver on the track. Someone also has to control the sled. This person is the sled operator, or driver. They sit in a special part of the sled and keep it in control.

# TEST DRIVE

THE SLED OPERATOR USUALLY
SITS IN A CABIN ON THE BACK OF THE SLED.

# ON THE TRACK

Truck and tractor pulls take place on dirt tracks. They are generally at least 30 feet (9.1 m) wide and 320 feet (97.5 m) long. However, that doesn't mean the vehicles drive the full length of the track.

# TEST DRIVE

IF A VEHICLE IS ABLE TO PULL THE
SLED TO THE END OF THE TRACK, IT'S CALLED A
"FULL PULL." THIS IS PRETTY UNCOMMON.

# NO NEED FOR SPEED

Unlike other motorsports, truck and tractor pulling isn't about going fast. Instead, it's about the distance, or how far the vehicle can go. To be a winner, you need to be a good driver and have a strong truck or tractor.

# TEST DRIVE

SOMETIMES THE WINNER
ONLY BEATS OTHER VEHICLES BY
A **FRACTION** OF AN INCH OR
A FEW CENTIMETERS!

# HOW IT STARTED

Before tractors, farmers used horses to pull machines. Sometimes they had competitions to see who had the strongest horse. Commonly, a barn door was fixed to the horse and people would jump on the door! The horse that pulled the most people the farthest won!

# TEST DRIVE

HORSE PULLING COMPETITIONS STILL
HAPPEN TODAY. HOWEVER, NOW THE HORSES PULL
WEIGHTED SLEDS INSTEAD OF PEOPLE.

17

As time went on, farmers started using tractors for work they once used horses for. Many farmers now wanted to see whose tractor was strongest! Tractor pulls were held as early as 1929. By the 1960s, they had become well-known.

# TEST DRIVE

ONE OF THE FIRST PULLING EVENTS THAT USED VEHICLES WITH **MOTORS** WAS HELD IN BOWLING GREEN, OHIO. TODAY, THE NATIONAL TRACTOR PULLING **CHAMPIONSHIPS** TAKE PLACE THERE.

# MAKING THE RULES

When truck and tractor pulls first started being held, the motorsport had no fixed set of rules. Each competition could be different, depending on where it was held. Sometimes, events nearby each other would even have different rules.

# TEST DRIVE

WITH SO MANY DIFFERENT RULES,
IT WAS HARD FOR PEOPLE TO TAKE PART
IN TRUCK OR TRACTOR PULLS THAT THEY
HAD NEVER BEEN TO BEFORE.

In 1969, a group of people came up with a uniform set of rules for tractor pulling. This group formed the National Tractor Pullers Association (NTPA). The NTPA is a sanctioning body. This means it oversees events and makes sure the rules are followed.

# TEST DRIVE

THE NTPA ISN'T THE ONLY SANCTIONING BODY IN TRACTOR PULLING. HOWEVER, MANY OTHER GROUPS FOLLOW ITS RULES, MAKING IT EASIER FOR PEOPLE TO TAKE PART IN MANY EVENTS.

# CHANGING IT UP

In the early days of tractor pulling, the machines were the same ones the farmers used for work. Over time, people started making changes to make their tractors even stronger. Today, tractors in competitions are very different from those used on farms.

# TEST DRIVE

FOR COMPETITION, PEOPLE GENERALLY FIT THEIR TRUCKS AND TRACTORS WITH VERY POWERFUL **ENGINES.** SOME EVEN USE ENGINES MADE FOR AIRCRAFT!

Since people make many changes to their trucks and tractors, the vehicles facing off are often very different from each other. For this reason, most pulls have different classes, or groups of vehicles that battle against each other.

# TEST DRIVE

MANY THINGS DECIDE WHAT
CLASS A TRUCK OR TRACTOR IS IN, SUCH
AS WEIGHT AND ENGINE TYPE.

# ALL KINDS OF EVENTS

Truck and tractor pulls are enjoyed all over—from small community fairs to big national events. Some places even have **remote control** truck and tractor pulls! People control small model trucks and tractors, making them pull a small sled.

# TEST DRIVE

IT'S COMMON FOR EVENTS TO SIMPLY BE CALLED "TRACTOR PULLS" EVEN WHEN TRUCKS ALSO TAKE PART.

# TRUCK AND TRACTOR PULL
# SAFETY TIPS

## TRUCK AND TRACTOR PULL DRIVERS SHOULD:

- KNOW THE RULES OF THE EVENT THEY ARE TAKING PART IN AND FOLLOW THEM.

- ALWAYS KEEP THE VEHICLE ON THE TRACK WHILE COMPETING.

- WEAR PROPER SAFETY GEAR, SUCH AS A HELMET AND CLOSED-TOE SHOES.

- KEEP A HANDHELD TOOL FOR PUTTING OUT FIRES, CALLED A FIRE EXTINGUISHER, ON THE TRUCK OR TRACTOR.

- HAVE A WORKING KILL SWITCH, A TOOL THAT WILL TURN OFF THE MACHINE IN CASE OF DANGER.

# FOR MORE INFORMATION

## BOOKS

Hoblin, Paul. *Tractor Pulling: Tearing It Up*. Minneapolis, MN: Lerner Publications Company, 2014.

Levit, Joe. *Motorsports Trivia: What You Never Knew About Car Racing, Monster Truck Events, and More Motor Mania*. North Mankato, MN: Capstone Press, 2019.

Weber, M. *Wild Moments of Truck Racing*. North Mankato, MN: Edge Books, 2018.

## WEBSITES

**Inside a Competition Tractor**
*science.howstuffworks.com/transport/engines-equipment/inside-tractor.htm*
Learn all about a truck that takes part in this extreme motorsport!

**What Is Tractor Pulling?**
*ntpapull.com/pulling-101*
Read more about tractor pulling on the NTPA's website.

**What Can a Tractor Pull?**
*wonderopolis.org/wonder/what-can-a-tractor-pull*
Check out this page to learn more about tractors and tractor pulls.

**Publisher's note to educators and parents:** Our editors have carefully reviewed these websites to ensure that they are suitable for students. Many websites change frequently, however, and we cannot guarantee that a site's future contents will continue to meet our high standards of quality and educational value. Be advised that students should be closely supervised whenever they access the internet.

# GLOSSARY

**championship:** a competition that decides which person or team is the best in a certain sport or game

**competition:** an event in which people try to win

**engine:** a machine that makes power

**fraction:** a part or amount of something

**motor:** a machine that produces motion or power for doing work

**remote control:** a tool used to control electronics

**steering wheel:** a wheel that a driver uses to control the direction of a vehicle

**vehicle:** an object that moves people from one place to another, such as a car

# INDEX